atlas
of
Feelings

notionpress
.com

atlas of Feelings

Pratik Agarwal

Notion Press

Old No. 38, New No. 6
McNichols Road, Chetpet
Chennai - 600 031

First Published by Notion Press 2016
Copyright © Pratik Agarwal 2016
All Rights Reserved.

ISBN 978-1-946204-64-6

CONTENTS

Contents

ACKNOWLEDGEMENTS

This book is dedicated to my parents, my brothers and the many friends who supported me on this beautiful journey and gave me the confidence to make a dream come true. I would also extend my gratitude to someone special who motivated me a lot. Without you all, writing this book would have been impossible. Thank you.

THE SPECIAL ONE

You changed my world with a blink of an eye
This is the fact which no one can deny
You turned me from the worst to the best
This is why in the whole world you are my dearest

You will never know what you mean to me
And our relation is such in which no one can else be
You are really an angel sent from above
You take care of me and shower your love

Till when you are with me I will not cry even a tear
Your delicate touch removes all my fear
Along with you living my life is worthwhile
And it turns more beautiful with your smile

It's so magical those things you made
You brought back my smile which turned fade
I realized that my dream has come true

It all began when I started loving you

You are the only one I can't even think living without

This fact is true and am sure there is no doubt

The first time I saw you I wanted to steal your heart

And thought will keep you happy and we'll never be apart

Along with you my life is totally complete

Our bond is strong enough which no one can defeat

You are my princess, my one and only

Give me yourself and I'll never be lonely

You are a true sweetheart, dear

My eyes keep staring at you when you are near

I keep searching for you in each and every street

And make excuses to everyone so that we can meet

Finally I found out what I was looking for

It was you, your care, your love, and nothing more

When you turn angry I know how to make you melt

Past several months those touch I have felt

I want to talk to you till the end of the day

But I am running out of words to say

I want to end the poem with the line you know

I love you more than what I show…!!!

REGRET

Neither in my life had I wanted to hurt you
Nor in the future I want to loose you
I know these days I turned mean
But I swear my intentions were clean

U seemed to be very angry I guess
So now it's time for me to confess
I am writing this poem for a cause
Those few days brought your life to a pause

I am really very sorry for the days I gave
For it I should be treated like a slave
I walked all alone looking at the sky
I didn't inform you because I didn't wanted to lie

It was the first time I have seen your anger
Which made me far and turned me a stranger

I realized I am incapable and even I am bad
Who always finds a reason to make you sad

I am not even worth of asking forgiveness
Because as usual I always create a mess
I am really very sorry for making you cry
Can't give back your tears but surely I will try

Everything all around seemed to be busy
Spending those few days was not that easy
I know those days was the worst for you too
But I swear each and every second I missed you

Turning a stranger for you made me weep
I know my actions hurted you deep
I can't stop thinking about you the whole day
And I know selfishness is on my way

I know it's a joke when I say sorry to you
I am becoming the worst and turning fade without you
I beg for forgiveness because I realized what I have done
I need you back and want to be there with you with each rising sun…!!!

LIFE

Life is full of ups and down
No one is happier than a clown
Every time it's isn't a bad day
Even the waves destroys the bay

People doesn't have time for known
And they say you are the one I own
They have made love a new game
Ruining down its importance and fame

Life is something we should enjoy
Playing games should only be a toy
Humans give it up so fast
Without imagining how beautiful was their past

Life is a sort of battle ground
Problems will be there all around

We should always be ready to face

The challenges that comes in between our race

Today we can't depend on anyone

People now a day carry an invisible gun

The gun rests itself on the shoulder of trust

And people can't be judged just from their upper crust

Believing someone now turned to be a 'Lol'

Even a kid gets irritated playing with the ball

People are being divided into different class

Life is turning to be an empty glass

We are like the branches of a tree

Moving like a bird which is free

Ultimate aim is to touch the sky

Rising up and going high

Humans are tending to become selfish

Begging to God instead of a wish

They want life to become much easy

Want to achieve their goal without being busy

Life is not always a sort of miracle
It should be balanced like a vehicle
We started increasing our demand
Living life is somewhat like a command

Life teaches us to smile and cry
And always gives chances for a second try
We should not easily loose our hope
And move forward like a rising slope

Life is something not to discuss
It is a challenge for every one of us
We can't just get it if once gone
I only learnt that it goes ON…!!!

MEMORIES

Memories are something very valuable
This is every human's asset
It is quite elastic and expandable
With many past and future prospect

It can be preserved in any form
No matter with what it is related
None can replace it or transform
As these are incidents that are belated

It is something that holds and binds us
From the events occurred in the past
It is moreover like stitches and cuts
And becomes reason for someone to last

It can't be measured in any terms
Nor it can be bought with money

It sticks to our mind like germs
But it's even sweeter than honey

Memories tells us about our yesterday
And reminds us of the time spent
It gives courage in every possible way
And rises hope for future event

Living our present would be harder
If these memories weren't along
People will speak with great ardor
About the memories they belong

Everybody wishes for a time machine
To take a glimpse of their memories
Elders want to see themselves as a teen
And youngsters want to forget their worries

Memories can either be good or bad
But they are still very memorable
By looking behind we should be glad
As these memories are so adorable

I can't forget any memories of mine

No matter how worst or best it was

Without them I know I won't be fine

And will bring the life to a sudden pause…!!!

FRIENDS

Life would be like an empty bus
If they wouldn't be around with us
They are someone on whom the entire life depends
They are none other than our friends

They guide us in each and every possible way
They can even be with us for the entire day
No matter how busy there schedule is
They'll be always ready to help with great ease

Making friends in life is really worthwhile
Bt the relations with them shouldn't be fragile
The presence of friends is very necessary
As they always teach us to laugh and be merry

They are form of blessings sent by God
They are creations for whom we should applaud

No matter sometimes how rude they turn

To make us smile is their foremost concern

They lend us their hand in every tough situation

They help us to get out of all the tension

Their presence in life can't b neglected

No matter in past, how worst they acted

Few of them ignore us and we ignore few

Life keeps going on and all friends r new

Life is changing with d change in trends

But living life is impossible without friends…!

NOT AS HAPPY AS YOU

Sometimes in life we feel so blue,
But someone, somewhere is not as happy as you.

Somewhere far at the border when a soldier sleeps,
Missing his loved ones he silently weeps.

Somewhere a mother painfully sighs,
Coz her new born baby didn't open her eyes.

Somewhere a poor dad silently cries,
When he sees his son begging for a bowl of rice.

Somewhere in an orphanage a little girl's sad,
When she misses her mom n dad.

So at times a reason to smile u may not have any,
Say to yourself that you're happier than many.

Coz life is beautiful and.

Its not always blue,

And someone, somewhere is not as happy as you.

A RESTLESS FRIDAY

It was Friday

I was feeling restless

With courage I woke up

And started creating a mess

Wind was blowing and

The weather was cool

Surrounding was asleep

So I thought of not going to school

Yes, I was sick

And My prayers were votive

Bunking my attendance

Wasn't my motive

I was turning low

and was looking pale

Colour turned blue

And body became frail

I didn't know

What should be done

Whom to inform

As there was none

I looked around with fear

And found myself alone

at night I was happy

And now the smile was blown

Presence of someone was wanted

Just by my side

Holding my warm hands

And lying beside

I was shivering with cold

Realizing I am having fever

Remembered my sweater

Made perfectly by a weaver

At this worst condition

My mother was missed

I wished her to be there and gently

My forehead would be kissed
Why did they send me
so far for my studies
I know that's for my benefits
But parents were my true buddies

I lay down on my bed again
Mind running full of emotions
I felt I was still near them
What about going across oceans
My health was turning worst
And then I decided to sleep
I crawled under the blanket
With a silent weep…!!!

FIGHTS DON'T LAST LONG

A cloudy night
With the stars shining bright,
Talking over the phone
I had a silly fight

I don't know what the reason was
Bt it did bring me to a pause
I disconnected the call very quick
And sat up straight with a flick

With this state so worse
I jumped onto my slippers
I stepped out in the lane
Without realizing about the rain

I looked up in the sky
And suddenly I started to cry

Very soon I was completely drenched
Shivering with cold, my fist, I clenched

Memories started running all over
I lay down on a sack of Stover
to me, she was very well known
Tears were rolling and I was all alone

Couple of hours simply passed by
And the tears finally turned dry
Then I decided to walk back home
Stepping on the fresh, fertile loam

I came back and took a great leap
Directly on my bed and soon was asleep
Night was a past and I needed to be strong
Doesn't matter coz fights don't last long…!!!!

DREAM

She went to sleep
closing her eyes
beginning to dream
of broken butterflies
tearing her lovely wings
on faithless love that angel sings…

She finds shiny metal in kitchen sink
in an evening absent light
she finds peace in cuts of pink
watching red blood flow feels so right...

Starlight shines upon her tears
I whisper darling, you cannot bleed
all of your suicidal fears

At night when you begin to cry

I'll sing you a lover's lullaby…

My love do not wish that you were dead

dreaming of an absent pulse

laying on silken sheets bleeding red

I will offer love so do not bleed

give me your knife I am all you need…!

AN UNKNOWN STRANGER

I saw a girl
Who was very cute
She was talking over the call
And her voice was like a flute
On noticing her deeply
She seemed to be worried
I think she was having a quarrel
With all her smiles buried

Couple of minutes passed by
And finally the call was ended
She was looking sad
With all her emotions blended
She sat down on a bench
With a deep sigh
Looked at her phone again
And began to cry

I wanted a smile on her face

With no single drop of tear

I kept staring for a while

And then finally went near

I sat beside her and

Kept staring into her eyes

Wanted to hear her problems
With no single lies

She looked at me strangely

And asked who I was

I said her my name and asked

"You look worried, what's the cause?"

At first she didn't answer

Just coz I was unknown

How long can you hold your feelings

And then she started saying looking at her phone

I kept hearing her

Without speaking a single word

And with no less time

Her story was getting slurred

After completing, all of a sudden

She busted out of tear

And hugged me as tighter as she can

As to her, I was only near

Realizing that I was a stranger

She quickly let me go

and then took a sigh

With the speed so slow

She looked into my eyes

And with "Thanks" she greeted

Then she carried her handbag

And stood up from where she was seated

I could see her going away

Without saying goodbye

And soon she disappeared

Leaving me under d evening sky

I walked back home all alone

Thinking about her all the way

I chanted a prayer n went to sleep

Waiting for a entirely new day!!!

I MISS A LOT…

I miss a lot, the long walk,

That seemed so short with you….

I miss a lot, the romantic talk,

Every word of which was true…

I miss a lot, the whole day

We used to together spend…

I miss a lot, the sunset ray

That we used to watch in the end…

But now all of it is past,

That is the sad part….

We both couldn't last;

We now have a broken heart!!!

This distance from you

Is something, I cannot bear…

I miss how you and me,

At each other would stare....

I wish that you come back to me,

That is what all I want...

I think I never deserved you,

Usually life gives me this taunt....

The day you will be back to me...

My angel! Nothing will be less,

My love, My care, My feelings,

For you will b everything immense!!!

YOU BOTH ARE BEING MISSED

I am crying a lot coz

Mom n dad you both are being missed

Mumma, Years ago you took a lot of pain

Tears were rolling down like rain

You gave me birth without caring about your cyst

I am crying a lot coz

Mom n dad you both are being missed

Dad, hearing about my birth, you were the happiest man

And just to see me, in a hurry you ran

Weeping, in your hand you took my fist

I am crying a lot coz

Mom n dad you both are being missed

You both enjoyed my childhood with fun

I hope one day you'll be proud of your son

I want to take your names high so that proudly you
can twist

I am crying a lot coz

Mom n dad you both are being missed

Dad, I remember how you used to hold my hand

My feelings, mumma, you always understand

Today I am pressurized and I'm completely pissed

I am crying a lot coz

Mom n dad you both are being missed

I really heart you both n this isn't a lie

Your orders, I promise, I'll never deny

If ever I go wrong, I want you both to assist

I am crying a lot coz

Mom n dad you both are being missed

For my mistakes, I beg, please forgive me

I'll forever serve you both, even on my knee

One day will surely fulfill all your wishes, do prepare
a list

I am crying a lot coz

Mom n dad you both are being missed

At your old age, I'll hold your hands, I promise you both

No matter how strong or weak will be my growth

Dear parents, I want my forehead to be kissed

I am crying a lot coz

Mom n dad you both are being missed…!!

THE REAL DIFFERENCE

Do you remember that day

Holding each other's hand

We promised each other

Not to be apart

In any case, in any circumstance

To be there with each other

In every situations

Sharing our smiles and

Wiping each other's tears.

Where is that friendship…??

Where it has disappeared?

Was I unable to stand

On all your expectations…??

Or you didn't ever bother about

My feelings, my friendship…??

Was I fake or
Wasn't I worth it…??

These questions surround me
Each n every single minute
I spend time thinking about,
The smile I wore just coz of you
I was fearless, assuming
That you were always by my side
I made mistakes just coz
I thought you'll be there
To guide me holding my hands

But you know what.??
I was wrong; completely wrong
"Promises are meant to be broken"
You proved this line to be correct
I was shattered by your ignorance
Tears kept flowing
Seeing you happy with your love.
I know you love him, so…??
Does it mean that his love
Is more powerful than my friendship???

If you think this, then you are wrong
Absolutely wrong…!!!!

I am waiting
Not for you to leave him
But for the time when you'll realize
The real difference
between Friendship and love
So that no other guy in future
Can be affected or shattered
By your ignorance, your friendship
And your FAKE promises…!!!

FAKE? NO!!

He is wearing a fake smile
Burying down his immense pain
He is slowly losing his life
And people call him to be insane

His health is turning to be worse
Each and every single day
He keeps crying the entire night
And sleeps with the sun's ray

He seems to be so happy
As if his life is full of glory
No one knows what's inside him
And no one knows his true story

His list of friends is endless
But none standing by his side

This is the reason why no one
Can see the tears he hide

Something is worrying him
With his present life running fast
He is of a talkative nature
But never speaks about his past

Ignorance by his close ones
Is making him feel all alone
He never complains about it
Making an unnoticed moan

To keep his own people happy
He does every possible thing
Still his relations with them
Is turning to be a broken string

He gives away his everything
To the person he really love
He demands nothing in return
Just the relation to rise above

He is completely pressurized
And his mind is full of stress

Still he do not plead for help
Coz he is strong, I guess

He is overloaded with emotions
But to anyone, he hardly shows
He dies everyday from inside
And naturally his pain grows

He is a die heart fan of roses
Not of any colour, but only white
He keeps on writing something
Not in the day, but late at night

He is innocent and he is true
For sure he has a pure heart
He has a lot of pain hidden
And he has been broken apart

Understand him, love him
But don't ignore him for god's sake
I know he wears a false smile
But definitely he isn't fake…!!!

FOREVER – A MYTH

I was so happy

With my life going so well

A part of it was missing

Which was later

Occupied by you

Yes its you…!!

Life became more happier

With your presence

Or I would rather say

A perfect one!!!

You picked me up from the bottom

Where I was lying insane

Completely numb

With none of my senses working

And then you

Taught me how to smile

With a broad

Really broad curve

I started to smile

With all my teeth being visible

Started laughing out loud

Until n unless

My stomach ached

I started to enjoy my life

With songs murmuring on my lips

You held my hand taking me through

A dense crowd of which

At time I was afraid of

You showed me a future

Of 'us' so bright

And then………

Then you just shattered it

In a go, like a kid breaking

A piece of glass with stone….

U left me there

From where you had picked me

And finally….

Tonight

I am left numb again

With tears rolling

Still visualizing n hoping

Of a bright future

Which you showed me……Of course!!

Of 'Us'…!!!

A NEW LIFE

Her voice made an echo
In between the four walls
As she was screaming
On top of her voice, which
Was clearly audible to the people
Passing by the room

They just passed that corridor
Ignoring the voice, coming out
Of that dim light room
As if they knew what was
Going in, behind the doors…

She was wet all over
With that salty sweat
Coming out of each and every
Single body part

She was shivering with

Vibrations all over

And her long pretty hands

Started to flapper

Along with her legs

Which was then grabbed

By strong hands and was forced

To stay still……

Very soon

Her scream diminished

And she laid there completely insane

With her eyes closing softly

With some drops of tear….

Her voice was slowly replaced

By a sweet amazing cry

Of a baby boy

Which she gave birth just

A couple of minutes ago

And that's how a new life

Came on this earth…!!!!

A CHANGING GAME

He had just heard your name

And he wanted to know you more

He started searching you,

Found you,

And you both became friends.

HE WON!

You both were friends now

And he wanted to know you completely

He started spending time on you,

Read you,

And you both became good friends.

HE WON!

You both just became good friends

And he wanted to come closer

So he started trying, to reduce

The distance,

And you both became best friends.

HE WON AGAIN!

As you both became best friends,

He had then fallen in love.

So he started exchanging

The emotions

And you both went into relation.

HE JUST WON AGAIN!

And when he is living for you,

You are making him feel alone.

So he started running away

From his life

And now your relation has no title.

Baby… YOU WIN…!!

SECOND FACE!

I made a blindfold
Over my eyes,
In the matter of trusting you
Just because, Dear!
U had a face so real,
So clean to be understood
At a glance…!!!

Days just slipped on
Along with several months,
And, I started coming
Closer, more closer,
And finally fell in love…
With the girl I trust…!!!

But now I feel so relaxed
So stress free…

Just coz I don't love you,

Anymore!!!

Thanks sweetheart,

For showing me your

SECOND FACE…!!!!

A PASSIONATE KISS

They stood up

And started to walk

Towards the ocean

Where,

The red sun was just about to

Touch the horizon

Of an evening so…

Romantic!!!

Holding each other's hand

With their footwear

On the other,

They kept walking with a smile

Until the silent waves

Touched their feet!!!

They stood there,

With both the pair of eyes

Staring at each other….

Their sandals slipped off their hands

When she rested her head,

On his chest so warm….

And with the half sun

Underneath the imaginary line

Where the ocean meets

The sky so beautiful,

Their lips tangled with……

A KISS so passionate……!!!!!

A SURPRISE SO ROMANTIC

He came early

Quickly cleaning the house

And prepared some supper

Sufficient for both of them

Maybe,

He is planning for a surprise

For his beloved…

Couple of hours later,

She entered a hall

Tired and exhausted,

Which was glittering with candles

And a table ready for dinner….

She took a sigh

When his hands came across

From behind…!!

The hug was romantic

And he carried her to the room

So that his un-rested wife

Can freshen up…

She started to change

In the surrounding so flirty

When suddenly,

He pulled her to the bed

Both lying side by side

With his sensual lips on hers…

The essence of love in the air

Made them intimate

With passion in the evening

So amorous…!!!

They went deep

With the running clock

And as the evening passed by,

She was found resting,

With her head on his bare chest,

And the dining table was left,

Untouched…!!!!

SHE MOVED ON...

She moved on

Leaving him behind

In a condition so worse,

That day by day

He declined…

She was trying to forget

The memories he gave

And he sits in the corner,

Like a sick

He behaved…

She was living

And continued to enjoy

Forgetting the way,

She played

With that human toy…

He kept ignoring

The calls from his mother

And his ashtray was filling
As his cigarettes was running

One after the other…

She became successful

In removing him from her life

And his nerves was waiting,

To be cut

By a knife…!!!

A STORY UNSAID

He is alive

With his soul dead

Behind it, is a story

Which is unsaid…

He used to spread smiles

With full of pleasure

But he himself,

Never made that curve…

He fought, on behalf of

All his close ones

But he used to stand alone

When the world was against…

He gave solutions

For everyone's problems

But his own queries

Were buried unsolved…

Tears of his loved one's

Were soaked by his handkerchief

But his own shedding tears

Made his pillow sodden…

He is left un-noticed

As if, his blood isn't red

He still has a story behind,

Which is completely Unsaid…!!!

A LONG WAIT

She started to read

A book,

On her couch…

Waiting for,

Him to call back….

He started to pour

The liquor,

In his glass…

Waiting for,

Her to call back…

And somewhere,

In between this…

She became a

"Bookworm"

And

He became an

"Alcoholic"

LOVE – NEVER ENDING

Their eyes made a contact

With each other's…

And

Within seconds,

Their hearts got exchanged…!!!

They met,

They talked,

They quarreled,

They laughed,

They cried,

And soon…

They kissed each other,

In front of everyone,

Inside a religious building,

Saying…

"Yes, I Do"

A FULL STOP

Our story was running well

A perfect love story…

With no tears,

With no fears,

When…

All of a sudden,

I fell ill;

I fell depressed,

And needed some rest…

SOME rest…

But darling,

You had no patience…

I had asked for,

A Coma…

And…

You gave it

A Full Stop…!!!

SOUL – SLOWLY BURNING

Many half burnt memories
Were thrown in inside…

Many half blown thoughts
Were lying side by side…

A small puff was inhaled
With every smile he lied…

A long puff was taken
With every tear he cried…

Soon,
The ashtray…
Was stuffed with buds…

And,
Without anyone's knowledge
His soul within…Has died…!!!

SMALL LITTLE WORLD

With the love,

In the air…

I want to walk holding your hand

Across a long, straight road

Which never ends

And

Which is even less travelled…

So that, we can proudly say…

Yes,

I have walked on a road,

Which leads to a new life…

A new place…

Having no fear in our eyes

Coz…

I was with my world…!!!

TURN BACK EMPTY HANDED

Come behind me,

Just to see how far I go,

How far I can run from myself…

Hold my hands

And

Walk beside me,

Take a glimpse of how I live my life,

Alone,

In a new world,

Where I can cry out loud,

And there is no one to listen to me,

A place where I can talk,

Talk only to my soul…

Then you may leave my hands,

And go back,

Empty handed…

Coz

No matter,

How much you request,

I will never come back…!!!

UNTOUCHED BOOK

Yes,

I am a person,

Who hide thousands of feelings,

Behind my fake smile,

That the world thinks to be true,

But…

It doesn't mean that…

I am selfish,

Or I am showing off my good nature…

Its just that,

I don't want my close ones,

To get tensed just coz of the problems,

That kill me every second…!!!

I just want to talk to someone,

For hours,

And open out my heart to them,

But then,

I find myself alone

And

There's no one to read a book,

Which is completely untouched…!!!

WORLD – A SHOW

Take me through a dense forest

Where I can just be lost

To myself

And stay away

From this world of cruelty,

A world full of people,

Holding masks in their other hand,

Running for a life,

Having no humanity…

I want to be there where birds sing love songs,

Where someone can smile

At your happiness

And cry,

In your sad times,

And where no one is even aware of the word,

Termed as FAKE…!!!

HEART ALREADY BROKEN

Take a close look

Into my eyes,

Stare at them

Until and unless I cry,

You will see the pain

I'm suffering with,

You will see the nights

I haven't slept…

But don't go too deep baby,

Or else you'll fall in love

And I wont be in a condition,

To break my heart again…!!!

THE BETTER ME

Today,

I am being judged

By the face I show…

And not on the basis,

On who I am…

But still I feel proud of myself…

Just coz I know the better me,

And not who the world thinks to be…!!!

A BLIND LOVER

Hold my hand baby,

For sometime,

Not forever,

Coz I know,

That wont happen,

Even if you make promises,

But still I want,

You to hold it…

Unless you are satisfied

And leave it in a go,

To be caught again

By a better person,

Than me,

But still I want

You to hold it…

So that I can learn,

Some lessons on betrayal,

Which I was unable,

To understand,

As I am blind,

Blind in loving,

The only girl,

I am in love with…!!!

ME & MY SOUL

My soul is yelling,

From within,

To escape this layer,

Of so called skin,

So that it can be free,

Of a life so worse,

And of course a life,

Full of curse,

It keeps hurting me,

Again and again,

To leap out of a life,

Full of pain…

But…

If my soul is obstinate,

Then I am stubborn too,

I want to live my life,

Accompanied by you…!!!

EYES SO TRUE

Look at me,

In a manner so strange,

Ignore me,

As better as you can,

Move on,

Forget about the promises,

Speak up,

Forget about the lies,

Laugh around,

Forget about the memories,

Keep smiling,

Forget about the tears…

No matter what you do,

No matter what you say,

Only your words can be fake

Baby…

But not your eyes…!!!

A COURAGEOUS LIFE

I started to walk,

Towards the edge,

Of that long cliff,

On the floor so high,

Thinking of ending my life,

Coz you made it sure,

That you can't be mine,

But then…

I just stepped back,

Baby you know why…???

Just coz…

There is no other reason,

To live a life,

Where you can't have the guts,

To see the person smiling,

Whom you love,

And

Think about,

More than yourself…!!!

HER GROWING LOVE

She started to love more,

Even after those tears,

Which she wiped off,

Every single night,

On her pillow cover…

She started to love more,

Even after those fights,

In which stood first,

Was their own ego,

Making it last long…

She started to love more,

Even after those pain,

Being repeatedly given,

Which she covered it,

With a smile so genuine…

She started to love more,

Which kept on growing,

With the heart-beat,

Beating so fast,

But unfortunately,

For someone else…!!!

SOUL – SO PRICELESS

I had a way,

Of getting myself back,

From things that have broken me…

I wanted to get my small little heart,

Definitely not fake,

To start beating back,

For the ones who deserve,

For the ones who care…

I knew it will be expensive,

But not beyond my limits,

But it asked for something,

Which was priceless,

Yes,

An another soul…!!!

YOUR VALUABLE SMILE

Break me dear,

To an extent in which

I'm unable to stand,

Put me in a state

So worse,

That I cry out loud,

And no one will

Just even care,

Leave me there,

From where no one

Returns back,

And turn out to be insane,

And completely destroyed…

Still I promise,

To come back,

With more courage,

Just to show,

I am living again,

Even after being broken,

Just to see you smile…!!!

AFFECTIVE PAST

I have done many sins

In my past,

I have been dragged down

Several times,

I have been betrayed in

Every relation,

I have been lied every time

I trust,

I have been made to cry

Behind every smile,

I have been cheated for

My loyalty,

Yes I am at a peak of success,

But relations killed my humanity,

Coz I always ran,

And I'm still running,

Behind things,

Behind people,

Who broke me up…!!!

A SUDDEN LEAVE

A day will come soon,

When I'll walk away

Leaving behind everything

I possessed,

Forcing you to turn back

And take a glimpse

Of the smoke that vanished

Making a deep impression

On the lives of people

Who just crushed up

The heart that cared

And I swear,

U wont be even getting

A chance,

To bid him a goodbye…!!!

A BURIED SINNER

His soul is buried in there,

Alive, with all his feelings

Inside a holy box,

Regarded as a coffin,

Entirely vacuum

With no single attempts,

Of escape to freedom,

Just to make him suffer,

Bringing it to his knowledge

That he is a sinner,

Just coz for,

Penetrating into a body,

So veracious…!!!

Printed in Great Britain
by Amazon